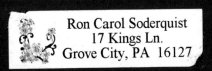

P9-APD-429

W9-CEL-115

Those Who Knew Him

Those Who Knew Him

Profiles of Christ in Verse

Gilbert Morris

Illustrated by Stan D. Myers

Fleming H. Revell
A Division of Baker Book House
Grand Rapids, Michigan 49516

Library of Congress Cataloging-in-Publication Data

Morris, Gilbert.
    Those who knew him : profiles of Christ in verse / Gilbert Morris; paintings by Stan D. Myers.
       p. cm.
    ISBN 0-8007-7155-9 (cloth)
    1. Bible. N.T.—History of Biblical events—Poetry. 2. Christian poetry, American. 3. Jesus Christ—Poetry. I. Myers, Stan D. II. Title.
    PS3563.08742T48 1997
    811'.54—dc21
                                         96-53602

Scripture quotations are from the King James Version of the Bible.

To my good wife, Johnnie
and
To my good friend, John Wink

Contents

Dawn

Now the birth of Jesus Christ was on this wise: When as his mother Mary was espoused to Joseph, before they came together, she was found with child of the Holy Ghost (Matt. 1:18).

Mary

Three days I've waited here, but Joseph's smile
Has silenced me. I could not speak my heart
Beside this sunlit well with strangers close.
But now so late he works the sky is veiled—
Except for rose-tints from the dying sun,
And even now they fade, I hear his steps;
Tonight I must tell him I am with child.

He is a child himself (Though older far
Than I) and nothing knows of woman's ways.
More like a father than a husband, Joseph
Seems to me. Could it be that God
Foresaw the peril of a younger man
(Blinded by a hotly jealous heart)
Gave me instead to one made temperate
By the slowing pace of older blood?

I see him now in those dark sycamores
Feeling his way along the stony path.
His is the right by law to cast me off—
But how I fear to walk this road alone!
O God, if Joseph will but keep me close
Despite the public shame—I'll say your hand
Has moved the two of us to your own ends!

Then Joseph her husband, being a just man, and not willing to make her a public example, was minded to put her away privily (Matt. 1:19).

Joseph

And so she is with child—and yet no guilt
Disturbs those eyes. Quiet as Galilee
On a stilly morn that face which first I loved
When I had buried hopes of wife and home.
Oh, many laughed, and others frowned at Mary
Tender as the grapes from Eschol—joined
To a gnarled time-weathered oak like me—
But they could never know the summer warmth
She brought into my barren wintry life
When to my awkward hopeless plea to share
An aging bachelor's meagre poverty,
Mary smiled and placed her life in mine.

But now they say (my family, friends agree)
She must be put away, her shame be known.
Can I tell them why this cannot be?
What would my Rabbi say if I revealed
My midnight dream and spoke of one who came
Clothed in burning light and breathed such words
That brought me first to desperate fear—then joy?
Oh, I am not fit to hear the word of God
Direct! At second hand I'd hear of him,
Enough to keep the law and let the scribes
Discover God's intent; I thought it safer
Always to keep Jehovah at arm's length.

Yet now the God of Abraham unveils
Himself to me—obey I must though doubts
Arise to cloud my heart with chilling mist.
They've come to me and whispered *Who are you
That God himself should put such treasure
In your feeble, awkward grasp?*

Who am I then? O God, I know not that
Myself! I'm just a man confused, afraid.
How easy life had been if God had not
Concerned himself to interfere and change
My fondest dream to fit his hidden plan!

Well, let it come, whatever shame must be;
I bear the half; for once a man has met
With God and touched the Maker of all heaven
He can't endure the tasteless work of earth—

The child is God's not mine, I'm put in trust
To keep through pain or joy, beloved Mary
And her child from heaven—so be it God!

And she brought forth her firstborn son, and wrapped him in swaddling clothes, and laid him in a manger; because there was no room for them in the inn (Luke 2:7).

Innkeeper

All right—all right! Don't smash the door!
    What's this you say? You want a room?
There is no room; they're on the floor
    As you can see by light of moon.
This whole town's stacked with Jews from every nation;
You should have made an early reservation.

Who's that behind you in the dark?
    Your wife? You say her time is near?
Well, I can tell you that's no lark.
    Why did you drag her here this year?
No! No! There is no room—but listen stranger,
You two can stay tonight in yonder manger.

Now, back to bed—it's cold tonight.
    That girl will freeze in that old stable!
There's some will swear I've been too tight,
    But I must do my business able.
My bills don't stop—not even for a birth.
Besides—that pair? Well, they're of little worth!

Star Chasers

(Shandor)
Look there ahead—our beasts will never climb
That rock-piled mountain road, and I myself
Have reached an end. My brothers, we have climbed
Too many hills. My mind is stunned by miles
Of lonely rocks and treacherous foreign rivers.
So we have tried too much—to fail such task
Is no disgrace; God ever had our best.

We've questioned rulers, men and even priests,
But still we prowl and limp these hills
Without one trace of any newborn king.
Few have done more—many have done less.
Let us return to family and home.
Our dreams were greater than our little strength.

(Melchior)
I, too, Shandor, would leave this quest.
Not that the way has grown too hard.
We must go back and never rest,
Put our theology to the test.
We need more light, more revelation,
A firmer grasp on divination,
That star above, so luminary
We'll study at the seminary.
This quest was but a learning tool;
We must go back again to school!

(Denar)
Lift up your heart, Shandor!
Lift up your heart, Melchior!
  O brothers,
We have tasted danger—bitter and sharp.
  But who ever found God
    Softly?
      Comfortably?
Lift up your eyes,
    My brothers!
We know enough already.
  God will silent be to us
  If we ignore our star.
Remember our joy
  When God lit a star
  In our eastern heaven?
And in our hearts
  God said to each of us:
    "Follow that star!"
My brothers,
  I will never stop—
    Let rivers, mountains sweep across
      My pathless way—
        I follow my star!

You will go on?
  Good friends, let us climb together
  Yonder hill—
    Shandor, what did they call that town
    Just over this steep range of hills?
    Let me think—
    Was it—
        Bethlehem?

And he [Herod] said, Go and search diligently for the young child; and when ye have found him, bring me word again, that I may come and worship him also (Matt. 2:8).

Herod

Centurion! Centurion! See here,
　　A message from the troops we sent to find
Those snoopers from the East—remember them?
　　"Where is the newborn King?" they asked—of *me!*

Those fools you sent have let them slip away
　　So now we must take measures desperate.
Take your troops to Bethlehem, kill every babe—
　　Oh, *spare* me your protest—you've killed before!

I've dealt before with this kingly infection.
　　Kill it not it spreads itself like plague!
And who'd be first to go if a Jewish king
　　Arrived? Me—then you—then Rome itself!

We'll crush this infant threat to Roman power.
　　I'll have his blood! Centurion—begone!
My name will live and long remembered be
　　When this child's name is wiped from memory!

Shepherd

Well, here's Jerusalem, and I am home.
That shop I left last year for good, will
Be my tomb. But then, it's not a bad old box,
And since I've done my fifty years and two
Enclosed within those peeling walls, just let
Them bury me right there when time wags out.

It's late, and there's my window in the shadow.
Almost I see myself spinning endless rugs
Forever there—but no, I need not see a ghost
So many stranger things I've seen of late.

Tomorrow Tychicus will jibe at me:
Well, well, our wealthy herdsman is returned!
But where's the gold those sheep were going to bring?
    He never understood it was not money
Which bade me close my shop, turn all my cash
To sheep, and drove me from my buried life.

My city-cluttered eyes I craved to rest
Just once on clear, unbroken, desert space
Sweeping off to hidden continents
While sweet, unbroken silence touched my ears.
    For months my eyes were washed by canyons burnt
To crimson cinders, daubed with smears of
Yellow blooms. I saw the searing pale-blue skies
Of noon grow coolly dark, then turn to sheets
Of purple silk across the glittering sky.

If I cannot explain my going forth
Much less then my return. For who'd
Believe I've seen the heaven peopled
Thick as Jerusalem itself at noon.
Shouting wildly *Glory to God in the highest!*
Oh, how that cry shook heaven, earth—and me!
Or who'd believe the brightest of the host
Gave me command: *Go find the Christ of God!*

I heard, obeyed, and stumbling on these legs
So shrunk with age, out-ran my lad until
We found the child, then breathless fell
Struck sudden dumb by what that stable held!
When we returned, the wild Judean dogs
Had slaughtered every sheep and every lamb.
So I am back. Tomorrow I'll begin
My little life, and so we will laugh. But yet

There's always this—it isn't every birth
That brings the angels overhead to shout!
    Some sheep I lost, but had I stayed for them
All else were lost—but now my treasure's sure:
One night—for just a while—I saw the king!

Morning

Baptizer

So now the Lamb of God is come, but I,
John Baptist, knew him not!
Since first Jehovah showed himself to me
I've stood hip-deep in Jordan's silt-brown stream
And plunged the penitents so deep their heads
Almost took root in sand, their flailing legs
Like scrawny weeds of papyrus in a storm!
  Sometimes my words cut and nearly stripping
Flesh from bone—even Pharisees
Cried out to be baptized! O, hypocrites,
Not Jordan's water, nor the ocean deeps
Could purify the stench of your foul hearts!
Your fathers slew the prophets; now you come
That I may feel the venom of your fangs.

A thousand days I've stood, and every face
I've searched, looking for the Lord's anointed,
But knew him not when first he came to me.
We look for our desires so hard, that when
They come to hand our eyes are fixed afar.
So yesterday he whom I sought
Stood quietly beside me in the stream
While busily my eyes touched every face
On shore. And then, I gave a sigh and turned,
But as I touched his arm my hand recoiled,

For there, one foot away, I saw those eyes
That I had seen in dreams since God
In deep Judean desert sealed my task.
At first I thought it could not be, for he
Was smaller than my thought of him—he stood
Beneath my height, his quiet eyes looking up
To watch my face. Confused, I cried inside:
How can I tower over God's own Son?
O, foolish thought! God ever did delight
In unexpected forms to pour himself!

When heart and earth at last stood still, I asked:
Why do you come to me? O, rather plunge
Me by your hand beneath the cleansing flood!
For deep in muddy waters, I had found
The purity of God's own righteousness.
He gave command, so deep in watery grave
I buried him. But then, I know not how,
As he arose, all noises seemed to fade
Like hum of bees in some far distant field.
But out of silence came a clarion call:
This is my Son in whom I am well pleased.

Out of the burning sun there dropped a dove
So white it glittered in the upper air
Like burning snow—until on him
I held with my arms he came to rest,
And then—I could not see to see.

So now, I've seen the Hope of Israel,
The promised one, resting in these hands.
But strange it is that he who made these hands
Should rest in them—that God should trust a man!

A few more days, and then I must decrease.
My task is now to point men to Messiah
As I have ever done. He will increase
Until earth's very stones will hear God's call:
This is my Son in whom I am well pleased.

And he [Jesus] was there in the wilderness forty days, tempted of Satan (Mark 1:13).

Lucifer

They call him "Carpenter"—but O, ye spheres
   I see in him mine ancient enemy
Made flesh! Thus now I race in full career
   Defeated by this one from Galilee.

How many dignitaries, prophets, priests
   I've lured up to temptation's razor edge
Then plucked them down to death without release.
   Now hear, ye hellish powers, my deadly pledge:

I'll empty hell! With demons fill the earth
   Until it cracks! We'll sweep on mighty pinions
Wreaking nature to untimely birth;
   We'll have this healer under hell's dominion!

What though he spurned my bread—my power—my glory?
When he lies dead, earth will forget his story!

And he ordained twelve, that they should be with him, and that he might send them forth to preach (Mark 3:14).

Disciples

O Sarah, look, there's the carpenter—
You know, the one from Galilee who's out
To save us all.
Better if he'd kept to mending chairs!
We get a bumper crop of backwoods prophets
Who've "heard the call" to lift us out of sin.
Out of this rocky ground that won't grow corn
Messiahs spring each year like bitterweed.
This Jesus is the latest, but he'll soon find
Men aren't as easy to repair as chairs!

Just look at them—his disciples there.
If this rabbi hopes to change the world
He'd better learn to watch his company.
That big redheaded one? Nothing but
A fisherman. He's loud enough to preach;
Tough enough, they say, to punch a head.
He won't save souls with noisy talk or fists!
Give him a month—glad enough he'll be
To get back to his nets again.
Men aren't caught as easily as fish.

You see those two? What tempers they both have!
Smash an oar to splinters in a rage
Just because of a missed fish or two.
No one would guess they're called the Sons
Of Thunder!
    Look right there—I'd heard the carpenter
Had called a tax collector named Matthew;
Well, won't that make the rabbi popular
With all the Jews who hate the name of Rome!
    Let's go, Sarah, this depresses me.
A foolishness, to call such men
From useful work—for what? They'll fail
Like all the others.
    What's that? Why, yes, he is the one
Exception in the crowd—see how fine he looks,
Just as a preacher should—and glad enough
That crowd should be to have a businessman
Like Judas there to keep an eye on things.

The ruler tasted the water that was made wine, and saith, Thou hast kept the good wine until now (John 2:9–10, author's paraphrase).

First Miracle

O child
  Of my virginity,
This water felt your touch
      And blushed to wine!

See how red it is,
  Like Sharon's morning rose,
    Yet clear as Hebron's streams
      It sparkles in my cup.

    O son of strangeness born,
Would that I could know your hidden heart
      As clearly as I see this clear wine!

    I think your days will be
A bitter draught of pain
        (which I too must taste)
A bitter drink and not sweet wine
      For Mary's son.

Alone that man must walk
Who touches water into wine—but then
      You always were alone,
        Not least in humming crowd, and yet
Your silence was companioned by
        Unspoken winds.

These have drunk your red, red wine;
But men were never satisfied
        By timely tastes.

O son of sorrow,
When these vessels emptied are,
    What wine must you pour
        From deep within
            To quench our thirst?

O son of man, what wine
At last will you pour out
        For us?

High Noon

And a certain woman came in the press behind, and touched his garment, and she was healed (Mark 5:25, 27, 29, author's paraphrase).

The Touch

Come, Jacob, see the breakfast I have made?
Hot bread and honey-cakes, ripe figs, and thick
Warm milk with rice plumped thick with juicy raisins.
O Husband, so many days I've watched you cook
While I lay sick, more your patient than your wife;
So now, to rise and fix a simple meal
For you—almost it seems I am a bride
A second time so strong and young I feel!
Was it but yesterday I woke
So drained and weak you had to hold my cup?
Now see how easily this heavy jug
I toss—O do not scold me—not today!
Since I touched his robe my whitened blood
Has flushed to scarlet (see the pulsing throb?)
Overflowed my heart and quickened like
Spring freshlets fed by drenching harvest showers.
Not so when yesterday I dragged myself
Through crowded streets holding to the walls,
And would have fallen, but so packed the street
Like close-set grain, we held each other up.

Then he came—the air so noisy grew
My voice was drowned like a cricket's chirp.
How did I ever have the strength to push
Myself between those bruising bodies, to reach
My stick-like arm until the tendons stretched
Like tensioned wire?
   I know but this: I touched his robe
More lightly than this breeze brushes my hair,
Just so—then muted all the clamorous noise;
A sudden force broke forth, the throbbing blood
Beat through my veins and drummed so loudly that
I almost failed to hear his voice:
"Daughter, thy faith hath made thee whole."
So strong the pounding of my blood I did
Not see him go, but in a silent street
I found myself alone.
But, Jacob,
How can we really be alone when God
Walks down our streets—
And lets himself be touched?

There met him . . . a man with an unclean spirit, And he asked him, What is thy name? And he answered, saying, My name is Legion: for we are many (Mark 5:2, 9).

Legion

He's squealing still? Beelzebub! So deep
    We pushed his mind to hellish dark
    You'd think his screams would be a tiny cheep!
I mind when first this vermin (for a lark)
    Grew curious, began to dabble
    With witches, warlocks, all that rabble,
    Charms, black mass he learned to babble.
Like Faust he uttered profane incantation:
We possessed him—at his own invitation.

First was I to seize his silly mind
    Followed by a hellish company;
    His soul we sucked dryer than a rind;
Hell laughed to watch his bitter agony!
    We drove him from his home and bed,
    Made a madhouse in his head,
    Drove him to live among the dead—

O come ye Powers, rip and tear and rend
This soul—let life for him be Hell within!

But halt, ye Principalities—'tis he!
  Such light! Our ancient adversary!
  Jesus, what have we to do with thee?
Come, hosts, in yonder swine ourselves we bury!
  I'm safe—but no, this piggish brain
  Whirls giddy round—the awful strain
  Of demon host gives too much pain,
Look out—that cliff—you're plunging o'er the side!
  I am unhoused—by churlish hogicide!

And when he was come in, he saith unto them, Why make ye this ado, and weep? the damsel is not dead, but sleepeth (Mark 5:39).

Strange Sleep

They will not ask, still
   I see the Question in each face:
     What was it like when you were dead?

My mother whispered once: "Jairus,
The child *was dead*—!" but Father
Stopped all talk from her and everyone
(Though he has questions, too).

   But I could tell them nothing
     They'd want to hear:
       No ghosts or spirits did I see.

I remember a fever
Burning inside
All mixed with chilling cold
That hurt like broken bones;
Something squeezed my head
As I have squeezed a grape until
Pain blurred every sight—

   Then the air turned sudden cool and still
   And the dark room began to glow
   Like old silver of the moon.

I rested in the cool light
   And listened to a strange song,
   A far-off song, clear and sweet
   Like distant mountain streams.
The words I can't remember,
   But they were both old and new,
      Without beginning, without an end.
A cool silver light,
A song without words—
   But then after all time and no time
   A voice, far off and strong:
Damsel, I say unto thee, arise.

The busy sounds came rushing back,
And I woke up to see a man
Holding my small hand in his large one.
            So it was.
I wonder if I ever shall again
   See that cool soft light: or learn the words
      To that far-off wordless song?

There came down a storm of wind on the lake; . . . And they came to him, . . . saying, Master, master, we perish. Then he arose, and rebuked the wind and the raging of the water: and they ceased, and there was a calm (Luke 8:23–24).

Storm Tamer

Man and boy I've fished this sea;
　　All weathers, foul and fair, I've known,
That storm tonight on Galilee
　　I say, was of the Devil blown!

It came too quick. Like a pack
　　Of howling desert dogs it slashed
Our sails to threads and then attacked
　　The ship as pale-green lightning flashed!

Look you at this hand that still
　　Is trembling like a wind-blown feather!
But yet, I did not shake until
　　The Master spoke—and calmed the weather.

Tell me, John, what manner of man
　　Is this, that howling winds grow mild,
And raging waves, at his command,
　　Quieten as a sleepy child?

And see how restfully he lies:
　　More placid than the chastened sea
His face; cloudless as the skies
　　Above—but who and what is he?

This storm, I'd say, is not the last
   We'll know—that's if we follow him—
He's one who'll draw the lightning's blast.
   Dark his path, and very grim.

But though my hands are shaking yet,
   (And may shake more another day)
This Jesus has me in his net—
   I'll follow in the Master's way.

There met him ten men that were lepers. . . . And one of them, when he saw that he was healed . . . fell down on his face at his feet, giving him thanks (Luke 17:12, 15–16).

Leper's Hymn

God in heaven!
   What is this glow of blood I feel?
My hands tingle—look you here—
Fingers straight and long,

      Not raw knobs of flaking flesh!

My face,
It burns—as flesh long frozen prickles into life!
Let me pull away these stiffened rags, there . . .
     O Mighty God, I'm *whole!*
No more this ravaged face
    With bloody flap for mouth
     And ragged holes for eyes,
No more this carcass of a face
Nibbled and torn by hooded vultures
    No longer frighten fear-stung child!

O Master,
The others go without a word;
    Forgive them, Lord;
So long they've tasted kicks and hate
    So long they snatched for crumbs
That they forget to kneel to God who heals.

You give me life.
My flesh has long my coffin been,
　　Entombed by peeling walls;
　　　　But deeper than my flesh
　　　　　Disease has troubled

Unclean! Unclean!
I have cried of corrupted bone, and flesh;
Unclean! Unclean! Cry I now to him who seest the heart!

Make now my soul as clear and pure
　As you have made my flesh, O Lord;
　　　If God Immanuel will touch the flesh
　　　　With healing hand,
　　　Does he not yearn to heal the
　　　　Sickness of our broken hearts?
　　　　　The hurt of every man?

And as Jesus passed by, he saw a man which was blind from his birth, and said unto him, Go, wash in the pool of Siloam. He went his way therefore, and washed, and came seeing (John 9:1, 7, author's paraphrase).

First Sight

In the pool of Siloam, he said, *go wash your eyes;*
    Well here I kneel to wash this crusted mud
Away—but I'm a fool to think this flood
    (Or any) could make me see the earth and skies!

And yet,—what *is* this tingling that I feel
    As I daub this tepid water? My face
Prickles as if a tiny wasp raced
    Across my lids with legs of springy steel—

O God! What is this burning in my brain
    Biting at my eyes—*it is the light!*
And now comes rushing in the world of sight
    Drowning me with flashing dyes and stains!

What is that? A thousand hands waving
    Wildly? A tree! Why did they never say
How beautifully it swells and gently sways?
    Or tell me of the blue sky's misty paving?

Look here, a fuzzy caterpillar I know
    By touch—but cannot name this flaming spot;
What color is this stripe that's almost hot
    To touch so sharp and biting is its glow?

I drink in sights as thirsty earth the showers;
   Too short our lives to see the world!
Let me see dogs, baby curls—
   Everything from dust to glowing flowers!

Why wait I here? Though every sight surprise
   And catch me off my guard with splashing beauty,
One thing I'd see that is both joy and duty:
   The face of him who gave me seeing eyes!

Peter said, Lord, if it be thou, bid me come unto thee on the water (Matt. 14:28, author's paraphrase).

Sea Walk

Look, Tullius, through the dungeon bars—You see?
Why, do not turn pale, I've seen a cross or two before,
My son—one particular cross I mind—
But, no matter now; tomorrow all will be well,
All will be well with me—at last.
   Why Tullius, you weep!
A Roman soldier weeping for a Jew?
Peace now—and think how gracious God has been.
Remember when you came to be my guard?
Ho, Tullius, how tough you tried to be—
Watching with your soldier's eyes, a sneer
On your young lips, Oh, you struck a pose!
And I? I caught you in my net as once
I caught the fish in Galilee;
My bait? I told you of the Master until
Soft grew that warlike eye, and slowly you
Were captured by his power—as I myself
Was caught by him, long before your birth.
                  You have been my lamp
In this dark place, for as I spun for you
My tales of Galilee of long ago,
How we walked with Jesus through the earth,
So *real* it seemed again!
   I am grown old, and tired, too, but now—
All will be well for me tomorrow.

What's that? Can I walk unaided there,
You ask? So far as to my cross?
Oh, son, more eager than you ever ran
To sweetheart I go for this last walk,
For there, all will be well for me—at last.

   Now, one last tale you'll hear:
Something came to me when you asked
If I could walk so far—I remembered
Suddenly a walk I had—Oh, such a walk
You will not believe!
   Ah, I see it all so clear, that time,
White sails blotted out by night-black skies,
Quick flashes of white waves around
Our little boat, all of us were scared
I tell you—then John called out:
THERE'S THE MASTER!

   He came, the master did, striding through
The darkness, right across the rolling sea
As if he walked a field of summer daisies.
Well, in those days, I—humph—well, I just had
To prove my courage, so I called out:
Let me come to you—if you are real!
Jesus stopped, gave me a little smile:
Come on then, Peter, he said.

Well!—what to do, eh, Tullius?
Nothing for it but to jump and go,
(So clear I see that night right now!—I hear
Almost the slapping of the waves against
My legs and smell the tang of ocean salt.)
    What's that?—Oh, yes, I walked
The sea that night, but not too far you know.
Just for a second I took my eyes off him
Then down like an anvil I went, would have drowned
But Jesus fished me out—
    It grows late, get you to sleep,
My little walk tomorrow? What then?
A few faltering steps, a pain or two,
And then, my faithful Tullius, why then
All will be well for me—at last.

Jesus taketh Peter, James, and John . . . up into an high mountain apart, And was transfigured before them (Matt. 17:1–2).

Transfiguration

Once a bolt of lightning caught me open-eyed:
    Like fiery lace it scratched across the skies
Like a hot-white arm of petrified
    Sun-fire that glowed like giant fireflies.

Just so this afternoon my eyes went numb
    When Jesus unexpectedly drew down
Into himself the blazing fiery sun
    Glittering like the diamonds on a crown!

His garments glowed like fleecy clouds ignited,
    Or like those peaks of frozen snow;
But earth has never seen such fire lighted
    Since God himself touched earth eons ago!

But now he wears again his homespun brown
    Instead of vibrant light. Yet still, I ponder
When next he'll call the host of heaven down
    And clothe himself in sun, and awe, and wonder?

A woman of Canaan came . . . and cried unto him, saying, Have mercy on me, O Lord, thou son of David; my daughter is grievously vexed with a devil (Matt. 15:22).

Demon Daughter

They said I had no right to throw myself
Before the Healer. Aye—it may be so;
Should I then have held my peace? Nay!
Too oft I'd seen from out my daughter's eyes
All hell flash out at me! I could not bear
To see her face furrow deep with hate
Nor hear her gentle voice croak with rage,
Cursing, raving with a foul demon's tongue!
    So I was driven, crazed with mother's grief
To one they said could cast the demon out.
—But when I cried to him, he only looked
Without a word. I longed to flee
Until I heard him say: *I am not sent
But to the house of Israel.* Cold words
That numbed my heart!—yet I would not be still,
But gathered all my courage again to call,
Help me, Lord!
Warmer grew his face, but still he said:
I cannot throw the children's meat to dogs.
    I have glimpsed a warming sun behind
Dark thunderheads, so then I saw his love
Gleam faintly, a glow beneath cold formality,
I held his robe and cried:
Lord, let me have whatever crumbs may fall!

A silence deep, then the Master said:
Woman, great is thy faith; from this hour
Thy daughter is healed.
　　That was all. But as I sit and watch
My daughter's eyes (no darkness there, quiet
As a summer pond at morn they are)
I ask myself, what if I had not cried
A second time, or yet a third?
Is faith but this—to cry and keep on crying
When first prayers fail? Aye, it must be so,
For now I think on it, his face
Showed pleasure most when I would not be quiet.
The Master's silence is an invitation,
Not rebuke. Aye, he throws a challenge, then,
To see how far we'll risk ourselves to him!

He cried with a loud voice, Lazarus, come forth. And he that was dead came forth, bound hand and foot with graveclothes (John 11:43–44).

Lazarus

Brother?—
I saw you leave
The feast and followed. Let me rest
Beside you; we'll watch the night wind weave
Into a bundle, like a silver nest,
Those feathery sleeves
Of clouds.

Lazarus?—
I have not spoken
Of the hour I stood outside your tomb,
Heard its silence by the Master broken,
Saw you born again from that foul womb
Wrapped in death's token,
Yet alive!

Four days!—
Why did he wait
Until in death's dark tide you drowned?
He only spoke, then death and fate
Slunk back to hell like coward hounds—
But why so late
Came he?

And yet—
Was it not best
That he should come when every hope had flown?
Only then, through such a bitter test,
Could we in his simple word alone
Find a perfect rest
From care!

Why fear?—
I think, my brother,
That we—like yonder star—grow stronger
When we rise above a dark cloud's cover.
Come then, let us fear the night no longer—
God's own hand is over
Every life.

And Jesus said unto him, Go thy way; thy faith hath made thee whole. And immediately he received his sight (Mark 10:52).

The Last Blind Man

One year ago it was, Passover time,
Right here I sat, blinder than Samson when
He laboured for the mocking Philistines.

I remember excitement in the wind,
A mighty prophet come to Jericho
They said, and when I heard how he did mend

All sickness, how I yearned to rise and go
To him! Instead I sat and dreamed
A hopeless dream that only blind men know.

But then the highway came alive and teemed
With noise and dust; I heard a cry
Ring out, and sudden in me fresh hope gleamed:

Jesus Christ of Nazareth passeth by!
Like a drowning man with one last call
Before he sinks, I raised a piercing cry

That stunned the crowd, and in that hollow pall
I heard a quiet voice, *Bring him to me.*
Casting off my rags, forgetting all,

Trembling, I came before him finally.
So quick it was!—he spoke, a rolling tide
Of light washed out the dark—and I could see!

I've seen a lot this year; trees like brides
So slender-tall, arrayed in gleaming white,
Dusty wings of moths, deep-scarlet dyed—

O, my eyes have drunk in dark and light
Like wine! But did you know I was the last
That from his hand received the gift of sight?

He healed my darkened eyes, and passing then
Went to meet with death. With my fresh eyes
I watched him die—then saw him live again.

Afternoon

The Price

Seeing you, my son, standing all alone
In growing dusk, is more than I can bear.
Your heart is heavy—yet you must prepare
To live life as a man, without a moan;
Every day for weeks you've gone to where
The Nazarene with his glowing eyes
Entrances you—why, even now you stare
As if you'd caught a glimpse of paradise.

Paradise? No, Mother, be content;
This very day I chose to live, not die.
The Rabbi's price for heaven is too high.
This solid earth must be my element.
Sell all, he said—but when I passed him by
A tear of purest rain shone in his eye.

Nicodemus

Once I swam beneath
Green-gold ocean streams clear as air.
Looking up through the sliding sea
I saw the underworld through a prism
That warped the sun into a cone
        Of wavering light.

Through swimming eyes
Came visions of an arching sky all
Shattered, broken into fragments of
Geometric glass. All was light, but
Only a labyrinthine pattern could
        My sea-dimmed eyes perceive.

Tonight, I saw
Another world besides my own that
Strangely glowed. It flashed upon my mind
As Jesus spoke of uncreated winds,
Of sunless light—and of a second birth
        Into a purer world.

As a breeze shifts
The glowering cloud so that we see far-off
Reflections of a light-paved world in space,
Then drops the veil—tonight the Master's words
Afforded one quick look into his coming
        World of light.

And, behold, there was a man named Zacchaeus, which was the chief among the publicans, and he was rich. And he sought to see Jesus . . . and could not for the press, because he was little of stature (Luke 19:2–3).

Sycomore Tree

Who's that? Who calls Zacchaeus?—Why, Nephew,
There you are, beneath this tree I've climbed:
Strange fruit on this old sycomore, eh, Micah?
A miserable old publican dangling
Like a withered time-burned grape.
Ha! I read your eyes: *The old man's cracked!*
I hope he made his will before he perched
Up there, blinking like a sun-struck owl!

Not mad, Micah—just a little desperate.
(Let us say I play the fool in age
Because in youth I never dared to dare.)
O Micah, you are a mirror! In you I see
Myself as I was forty years ago—
Face set for getting, grasping, keeping!
No time for dreams, or friends, or joy!
It was those barren years that put me here
Risking my brittle bones up in this tree.

Would you believe I'm here because I'm lonely?
What's that? I'm too rich to be lonely? Fah!

I'm so rich my soul can taste the bite
Of poverty so deep it starves my soul!
My early hopes have twisted into nightmare
Shapes that mock me day and night, laughing
At my empty yesterdays and dark tomorrows.

Why am I here, Nephew? Laugh if you will,
But by this tree must pass the prophet, Jesus.
By the synagogue I heard him preach;
My prisoned heart opened like a door,
Loneliness faded like a mist.

And so, I ran ahead, and now I wait.
Yet—it is a foolish hope; why should
God's prophet look at me, a publican?
When last did I see love in any face?

But see, he comes, Micah!
At least I'll see his face—but everything
I'd give if this man Jesus would simply stop,
Look up, and with a smile,
Fill up this empty, frightened heart!

Living Water

Strangely still is Jacob's well, and deep.
                        See, I drop this pebble—
    There—hear that ghostly echo far below?
        I've dropped both stones
                And secrets here.

But you are
Silent.
      Quiet as
A sealed priest.
          When I was green with youth, my innocence
    You breathed, clear, pure as your own waters.
        But Time,
      (That ever spoils the fruit)
          Bruised me with his careless hand.

Dark, Oh dark
My harvest then;
Shames I could not whisper into your dim recess;
My woman's guilt fed
      In bitter silence on
           Itself.

But yesterday
Right here beside this well,
        Eyes I looked into
    Deeper than your hidden waters,
            And yet so clear, I saw
An ocean of pure love.

  I have seen
Within a prophet's eyes
        Myself.

    How strange,
  That we must see our shame
        Clear as the sun
  Before our souls be clean!

        O
    Well of Jacob!

        Sweet and clear your waters
    But
  I have tasted vintage now
        Immortally brewed.

Living water! Only let me taste forever from your cup,
    Oh, quench eternally my soul's great thirst!

Woman, where are thine accusers? Hath no man accused thee? She said, No man, Lord. And Jesus said unto her, Neither do I condemn thee; go and sin no more (John 8:10–11, author's paraphrase).

Adulteress

So short my breath—my heart pounds harder
Than old Simon's hammer on his anvil!
They meant to stone me,
Yet some of them I've seen before
(Less concerned with Moses and the Law!)
Old Eleazar—see how blue and bruised
My arm where he struck me—
Him with his pious talk, *Adultery!*
In the very act!
I could tell a thing:
His hot eyes I've seen glittering
When he came scratching at my door—at night!

Still, it was not me they hated, but *him,* the Rabbi
They brought me to.
Round him they circled—hungry-eyed, snapping
Like a pack of angry wolves!

When they snapped at him: *Moses said to stone her,*
What say you? I squeezed my eyes in fear;
One word from him—one little word—
Well, I'd be meat for wild dogs right now!
But then so quiet and still it got

I raised my eyes, to see him stooping,
Writing in the dust—right here you see these marks?
Since I cannot read I only guess
What sent them flying, guilt in every face.
The names, perhaps, of those who pray so loud
On Sabbath—then whisper in my ear by night?

But still I couldn't move until
He said, *I don't condemn you:*
Go and sin no more.
I saw him smile, and then—
He went away.
Now I sit and wonder of it all.

If I am to do as he commands,
O God of Israel,
You'll have to push and shove me to another life!
But if this man can save me by a few marks
In a dusty street,
Somehow I feel my life is safe
For all my days!

And Jesus went into the temple of God . . . and overthrew the tables of the moneychangers, and the seats of them that sold doves, And said unto them, . . . My house shall be called the house of prayer; but ye have made it a den of thieves (Matt. 21:12–13).

Dove Seller

Thirty-seven years I've sat right here and sold
These gentle birds,
Thinking it a service to Jehovah.
'Tis not the service of my childhood dreams,
For always I longed to be a priest,
To stand inside the veil and breathe
Rich, heavy incense while chanting
Holy prayers by the glittering light
Of the seven-stemmed menorah!
How wonderful to meet God face-to-face—
As Moses on Sinai's smoking crest—and talk
With the Eternal as a man talks with his friend!
But God holds some men at arm's length, while some
He better loves and whispers in their ear.
Oh how I longed to be God's favorite!
All through my youth I haunted this temple,
Begging God with tears to take me in;
Then, I saw that I was born to know
At second hand my God, not face-to-face.
So, I sell doves—no closer can I come
To the most holy place.

Cut my prices to the bone, I have,
So that the very poor can sacrifice;
No sick or cripples, but only perfect birds
Has been my boast (though it has kept me poor).
I'd thought that even this small service
Might pleasing be to God—

But when the prophet swept like a wind
Through the court today, I was paralyzed
By his slashing words. What did he say?
You have made my Father's house
A den of thieves!
I saw him there, whip in hand,
Coins tinkling on the floor like golden rain,
Doves from broken cages
Rising like a cloud of feathered smoke—
His eyes were smoky, too—like the fiery cloud
That burned on Sinai's top!
But I fear he broke more than my dove cages;
Easy enough they are to mend. But
What can heal my troubled spirit?

For when he said *My Father's house*
Suddenly I visioned this temple's glory,
Glory, that is, through God's own eyes.
A place of quiet peace
Bathed in the pure shekinah light
And ever the murmured prayers
Rising clean; sweet smelling
As honeyed incense floating up to heaven.
Then—I saw the ugliness that was:
Moneychangers babbling, screaming sometimes
Like yapping desert foxes,
Stink of bird droppings everywhere,
All noise and violence and trade—
No better than the profane market street.
O, if *I* grew sick at heart,
How must Jehovah grieve?

Well, I'm old to learn my lesson.
Wasted years I can't wipe out, nor heal
My memories.
Still—
Something to discover God's purity!
Something to glimpse even near the end
God's bright truth unhidden, unveiled
Beneath our dark disguise.
Something, I say,
To catch a faint glimpse
Of God's own light!

[He] saw the rich men casting their gifts into the treasury. And he saw also a certain poor widow casting in thither two mites. And he said, . . . this poor widow hath cast in more than they all: For . . . she of her penury hath cast in all the living that she had (Luke 21:1–4).

Widow's Mite

This year, Bartholomew,
you must begin to take your father's place,
young as you are. But do not fear; God's grace
so strongly moves and guards his own that you
and I can trust (like sparrow in the air)
    Jehovah's care.

Today you make the gift, my boy,
your father always gave with such delight.
Here is the offering—take these two mites,
put them in God's treasury with joy.
He alone who gives without a sigh
    hears God's glad cry.

I see you are in doubt—
you ask why we must give God everything,
the last coin, the total offering,
keep nothing back, leave not a farthing out?
Others keep back part; how is it fair
    that we (so poor) should dare?

We cannot afford
(as wealthy ones) to offer God a part.
Those who nothing have, with open heart
must gamble everything upon the Lord,
trusting God, as a bird his wing
      for everything.

      Be God's reckless fool!
Go to the edge of all the light you see,
then take another step!—Oh, surely he
who makes the rolling earth his round footstool
will suffer not that daring child to fall
      who gives him all!

Then were there brought unto him little children, that he should put his hands on them, and pray (Matt. 19:13).

The Blessing

O little ones,
May your eyes behold God's buried beauty.
May you see in twisted desert thorn
As in the fire-splashed rose my Father's touch.
The scorpion's arching curve, the dove's soft eye,
Armored claw of eagle, velvet dress of lily—
All, all are his design.

May your ears be tuned to hear
God's hidden melodies.
While others strain to catch
Sounds of clinking coin and pleasure's din;
May you hear unspoken, unsung hymns,
Those soundless pleas from heavy hearts.

Your cup of bitterness, even this I bless.
Child of Adam,
May earth's bright poison
Sweetened be, purified by love
Both human and divine.

Your pilgrim way I bless with light
Down all your days of wanderings dark,
Until you walk by light
Not shed by any sun create.

These tiny hands I bless;
Be strong for God,
Be tender for the earthly task.

May you be sheltered from the storm of sin,
Safe from sucking undertow of earth's delights.
Yet when beaten to your knees
By foes of flesh or air,
May you in finite weakness
Grasp the infinite God of strength.

Into your emptiness may God himself
Be poured, until
In your own flesh
God's spirit rear a sacred citadel.

Then took Mary a pound of ointment of spikenard, very costly, and anointed the feet of Jesus, and wiped his feet with her hair (John 12:3).

The Ointment

Now the eyes of Judas glow at me
Like dingy silver coins sunk in murky depths.
When I anointed Jesus and the oil
Ran down his feet like fragrant tears
Turned golden by the flickering amber lamp,
He snapped: *The poor will not be clothed*
By foolishness like this!
Harsh truth I tasted then,
And wished my sacrifice undone,
The oil unpoured.
But—must we *always* give by calculation
Paying love's installment piece-by-piece?
Were I lost in burning desert sand
With a single cup of brimming water,
Not in tiny niggard sips I'd drink
But in one wild excessive draught
Bankrupt my store!

At least one memory I'd have;
Let me be this once intoxicated
With too great love!
Better one brief orgy of devotion
Than minor sips
That leave us thirsty still!
Love that will not recklessly be spent
Leaves no fragrance—
So let me be poured out
For him like priceless ointment!
O let me emptied be—that love may come
And fill me full again!

Twilight

Jesus took bread, and blessed it . . . and said, Take, eat; this is my body. And he took the cup . . . and gave it to them, saying, Drink ye all of it; For this is my blood (Matt. 26:26–28).

The Last Supper

NATHANIEL

Why is this night so dark and sinister?
Why does the Master talk of drinking blood?
Where is Iscariot sent to minister?
Why sinks my heart beneath fear's rising flood?

THOMAS

This room
To me
Is thick
With doom.
Why is
My heart
So filled
With sad
Remorse
And dead
Regrets?

MATTHEW

And now—Passover night—
Lamb's blood upon the door
Softens God's fell sight.
We are redeemed once more!

JOHN

as i lie here upon his breast
time and care and every mortal fear
have passed into the west—
but why, on jesus' face a tear?

PETER

HE SPEAKS OF LIFE
BUT EVER SINCE HE CAME
TO EAT THE BREAD
TO DRINK THE WINE
I HAVE SEEN DEATH
FILL UP HIS EYES.
WHY CANNOT HE BE
CONTENT TO HEAL?
TO TEACH? WHY RISK
ALL POPULARITY,
SUCCESS AND GAIN?
BUT NO! HE ALONE
MUST GAMBLE EVERYTHING
FOR SOME UNCERTAIN
VAGUE AND DOUBTFUL PRIZE!

Foot Washing

When Jesus stooped, Bartholomew,
To wash my feet, the sight of him kneeling there went through
    My very heart! He's in some kind of prison;
    Almost it seems his soul is sick to death.
Quiet he is tonight, as if some fatal vision
        All but stopped his living breath.

        Have we grown tired of daily wonders?
Too many miracles numb the heart (as thunders
    Startle first, then petrify the fragile ear)
    And yet when first I saw a milky eye
So sudden at his word turn dewy clear,
        Remember my wild cry?

        This miracle we've seen tonight
(God's Messiah kneeling humbly in our sight
    Washing grimy feet) I never can escape—
    A love so strong it dares to don humility,
To make of it a royal cape,
        Why—that's miracle enough for me!

And they came to a place which was named Gethsemane (Mark 14:32).

Some Deadly Grief

Some deadly grief the heart cannot contain.
See there—that bloody sweat on Jesus' face!
Each man must taste a secret bitter pain.

Why groans he so tonight? Is it not plain
He's tormented by a fear he can't erase?
Some deadly grief the heart cannot contain.

From whence this sweat, these drops like bitter rain?
Are we to learn (in this dark place)
Each man must taste a secret bitter pain?

Pale he is as one who has been slain;
Wild his eyes as one by demons chased!
Some deadly grief the heart cannot contain.

He's loved too much, too much! Love has drained
Away his life, cut short his daring race.
Each man must taste a secret bitter pain.

His agonizing grief I can't explain.
What mean these tears, these groans—from him so chaste?
Some deadly grief the heart cannot contain.
Each man must taste a secret bitter pain.

He [Judas] came to Jesus, and said, Hail, master; and kissed him (Matt. 26:49).

The Ballad of Iscariot

O what do you here, Iscariot?
  O what do you here this day?
I seek a refuge from that sun—
  God's burning eye above.
To earth-deep darkness I must run
  Far from God's fierce love.

O where have you been, Iscariot?
  O where have you been this day?
Far off and far away I've gone,
  So far I can't return.
I am as barren and alone
  As star that ceased to burn.

O what did you see, Iscariot?
  O what did you see today?
I saw three crosses mar the sky;
  I saw the ruby blood;
I saw death dull a monarch's eye;
  I saw hell's darkling flood.

O what did you hear, Iscariot?
  O what did you hear today?
The thud of hammer on a nail
  Beat against my brain;
I heard a woman's rising wail
  Like ancient earth in pain.

O what have you done, Iscariot?
  O what have you done today?
I've sold the goodliest one of all
  For bits of blackened silver;
My life, my soul, they now must fall
  Into a hell-bound river.

O where do you go, Iscariot?
  O where do you go today?
To go to fierce and darksome ground
  I go to find my place;
There I shall hide in a dull mound
  Away from God's good grace.

Then Simon Peter having a sword drew it, and smote the high priest's servant, and cut off his right ear. . . . And Jesus . . . touched his ear and healed him (John 18:10; Luke 22:51).

The Ear

They bring the Nazarene in bonds
For you to judge, Lord Caiaphas.
But I, your servant, caution you
Be not deceived; for in the garden
When he stood ringed by his foes
Like a stag by snapping wolves,
Why, Sir, *he* was free while we
Were captives made by his mere word!

Nay, Lord, you know full well I'm not
Impressed by country carpenters.
You trusted me to whip the mob
Into a killing fit before
The Galilean charmed them
With his honeyed words.
Well, he had no chance to speak;
We swarmed the garden like wild bees
Our stingers out, our voices shrill!
All of his disciples fled—
(All but *one* turned pigeon-hearted!)
This one (a red-haired hulking brute).
Whipped out his steel and switched my ear
From off my head like a ripe grape!

I felt a chilling cold; the blood
Rivered down my face—you see
This stain, still damp and red?
So it trickled down my cheek.

My ear is there, you say? In that
You speak the truth, but *how?*
Why sir, the Teacher simply touched my head,
And as the water closes swift
Upon itself when slashed by stone,
My ragged flesh closed smooth and clear.

Be cautious, Master, how you judge
This man. If he can mend an ear,
Why then a soul, and if a soul—
Why, can he not heal all the world?
God guide you, Rabbi Caiaphas,
To see this man through God's own eyes!

Now Peter sat without in the palace: and a damsel came unto him, saying, Thou also wast with Jesus of Galilee. But he denied before them all, saying, I know not what thou sayest (Matt. 26:69–70).

Denial

He's dead, then, the carpenter from Galilee?
Well—Jerusalem can have a little rest
Now that he's safely crucified. No more
He'll spread his doctrine like the plague!
His ragged band—how many died with him?
What! Not one of them went with him to the cross!
They realized this Jesus cost too much!
These new religions come like ocean tide,
And when the tide is out every shrimp
Can have his day—but when the waters rise,
They scuttle to the first convenient hole!

That night I saw one here, right by that wall.
A leader of the twelve, or so they say.
You know, the city was bewitched that night!
Soldiers, priests, everyone roamed the streets,
And when they took the carpenter away,
We made a fire and ate and drank and laughed
As if it were a holy day somehow.

I saw him wander by and warm his hands,
And then I gave him to the hungry crowd:
He's one of them, I said, *a Galilean!*
Like a pack of wolves they turned on him,
Until he cursed and swore he knew no Jesus.

Then, rising high above the noisy mob
From somewhere far away, a cock began to crow.
Like a magic horn it pierced the air,
And like a sword it cut the fisherman's curse!
A tide of white swept up his reddened face,
He seemed to shrink, then fled the fire's light
Stumbling into darkness with a hollow cry.

Well, the carpenter is dead. What use
To keep a vain pretense? When dreams die
The dreamer has to die a little, too.
I think I'd choose to perish with my dream
Than live and breathe—without a dream at all!

And as they led him away, they laid hold upon one Simon, a Cyrenian, coming out of the country, and on him they laid the cross, that he might bear it after Jesus (Luke 23:26).

Because My Skin Is Black

What burden do you carry on your back?
Because Messiah fell beneath its weight,
I bear the cross—because my skin is black!

These Romans! They know how to crack
The lash on dark-skinned slaves of state.
What burden do *you* carry on your back?

When Jesus fell, the Romans saw the pack
Of faces and chose my visage dark with hate.
I bear a cross because my skin is black.

For us with sun-dark skin there is no lack
Of masters quick to pile us high with freight.
What burden do you carry on *your* back?

Yet when Christ looked at me that day, he lacked
No love for skins like mine, as dark as fate;
I bear a cross because my skin is black.

To bear his cross became a joy in fact,
So now I bear his cross inviolate!
What burden do you carry on your back?
I bear a cross because my skin is black!

And when they were come to the place, which is called Calvary, there they crucified him (Luke 23:33).

Nails

You see this forge? For twenty years
    I've beat raw metal into form;
How many two-edged swords and curving shears
    And shields were on this anvil born!

This dagger—look you how the steel
    Is married to the brazen haft
So smoothly that you cannot feel
    A line where blade slides into shaft!

To do good work has been my pride.
    I've been a father spawning life,
And this hot forge—my iron bride!—
    Has given birth to scythe, to lance, to knife.

But—since the day that Jesus died,
    My heart's been bound in iron bands.
I think of him—the crucified—
    I made the nails that pierced his hands!

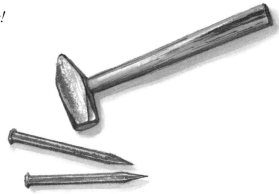

And he said unto Jesus, Lord, remember me when thou comest into thy kingdom. And Jesus said unto him, Verily I say unto thee, Today shalt thou be with me in paradise (Luke 23:42–43).

Dialogue of Death

(First thief)
Well, he's dead—your precious Messiah!
Where are all his fine words now?
Where's that paradise he promised you?
They're all alike, these would-be kings!—
Believe in me! They bellow—
I'll give you everything you need!
Then, you wind up in a torture chamber,
Or spilling your guts out on a cross, like us!
Where are all the fine, beautiful words now?
You can't live on words, I say!

(Second thief)
Yes—he's dead.
I knew he was dying like us.
But, don't ask me to doubt his words!
As I slip slowly out of this body
I can see so clearly that we live by words!
What use to me now of earth's vain food?
Women, wine, pleasure—they're all like ghosts somehow!
Fading into nothingness.
But his words—they're getting louder
Can't you hear his words?

Why, I hear them ringing like giant bells
Tolling in the air:
This day! I hear them toll,
In Paradise! they ring,
With me! How they fill the air!
This man was no false king!
They take the gold and run.
I hold his word as true—
Because he *joined* us—even in death!
And that's why he could say
Come with me—Come with me to Paradise!
Only a real king
Invites a beggar
To become a prince!

The governor answered and said unto them, Whether of the twain will ye that I release unto you? They said, Barabbas (Matt. 27:21).

Rondel

I missed my rendezvous with hell—
They slew the Christ instead of me!
As Jesus hangs upon a tree,
Barabbas leaves the prison cell.

That mob condemned with hateful yell
Their own dark souls eternally.
I missed my rendezvous with hell—
They slew the Christ instead of me!

This world's an obscene citadel
Built of shame and infamy!
How else explain such mockery?
They traded Christ for a criminal—
I missed my rendezvous with hell!

And when the centurion, which stood over against him, saw that he so cried out, and gave up the ghost, he said, Truly this man was the Son of God (Mark 15:39).

The Seventy-Third

Rome has so many ways to let out life,
And I have seen them all so many times.
Crucifixion is the current thing,
And seventy-three non-conformist fools
I've helped from this world to the next.
And seventy-two of these were all the same:
Young or old they irritated Rome
Sufficiently to get themselves nailed to a cross.
Oh, some had a certain *style,* as you might say.
I remember one—a thin Egyptian priest—
He painted his entire body a brilliant green!
(Which clashed with the scarlet of his blood!)
Some cursed, some repented magnificently
Rending the air with eloquent phrases!
But for all these eccentricities
Crucifixion is a monotonous affair,
So dull that seventy-two I've put to death
Flow together in my memory
Overlapping hazily and vague.

What's that you say?—Oh, yes, there *was* that one.
He seemed much like the others at first,
And all the cast was there—weeping mother,
Loving friends, bitter enemies,
Sight-seers—I'd seen them many times before.
There was the usual horror with the nails,
The customary sickening sounds of tearing flesh,
No different from the rest we've crucified,
And then the long silent wait for death . . .
Well, I thought, *That's one more,* and dozed awhile.
But then—he said some things, not very much:
Father, forgive them; they know not what they do.
To some young man he gave a charge—his mother,
As I remember. Once he asked for drink.

But, he spoke so quietly and with such certainty,
Like a general who knows his rank.
Well, he was *unusual,* to say the least,
But then it happened—I say he did not die!
Death takes men as lions take down the deer—
Grabbing with claws and dragging us to dens
Fighting, screaming, grabbing at straws!
But this man!—Why, he held death at arm's length
As with contempt I've made men cool their heels
Until I designed to let them enter in!
Then he said at last, *It's finished.*
And then he gave himself to cringing death.
All heaven broke loose with raucous wild applause.
Some said Thunder! I said that it was God!
That lightning was God's flashing grin!
The thunder was his rolling laughter!
The earthquake was his pounding hand!
And earth, the grave, the devil, and all hell
Can never hold this one—not *him!*
I say something was bound up when Jesus died—
I say something was set loose on earth that day!

Joseph of Arimathaea, an honourable counsellor, which also waited for the kingdom of God, came, and went in boldly unto Pilate, and craved the body of Jesus (Mark 15:43).

Lost Causes

Pilate!
Give me the body of Jesus!

You are surprised
That I, Joseph, can be so bold?
You must take it as you will—
And well I've weighed the danger
Of showing interest in a messiah—
Even a dead one!

Give me his body, my lord!
You have washed your hands
Free from his blood.
Well—perhaps you will sleep well,
Perhaps (like Herod) you will have bad dreams.
I speak plainly, do I not, my lord?

Give me the body of Jesus!
Oh, I was never the man for lost causes,
No, not Joseph of Arimathaea,
The careful Joseph, the cautious one!
Lost causes have a certain attraction
For romantic fools—But they always lead
To a grubby, tasteless finale.

So, I am become a romantic fool
Like all the rest that heard his words—
Even worse! For they have circumspectly
Cut their socio-religious ties with him
While I stand before the Roman governor demanding:
Give me the body of Jesus!

Lost causes bore me, Pilate—
But, I have of late
Become aware that life's little certainties
Turn the soul to mush—

So, like the fool who throws himself
In a wild, useless, and flamboyant gesture
On the points of some merciless phalanx,
I throw myself on you, Pilate—and on Rome:
Give me the body of Jesus—the Christ!

New Dawning

Now when Jesus was risen early the first day of the week, he appeared first to Mary Magdalene, out of whom he had cast seven devils (Mark 16:9).

The Ballad of Mary Magdalene

I have come with the myrrh and the aloe;
I have frankincense, saffron, and camphor
To anoint the dead Christ—yet I know
All their sweetness combined can't rekindle the fire
That once burned in his eyes, or restring the lyre
Of his voice that commanded the sea!
His body lies there clad in Death's grim attire—
But where is the Christ who set me free?

Soon the eagle of dawn will arise
And devour the carcass of night.
But where is the one who can exorcise
A demon of doubt who drowns all the light?
O God! How my heart feels the bite
Of a deathly fear from my ancient enemy—
The seven that he with a word put to flight—
But where is the Christ who set me free?

There's the sun—how it lights up the tomb!
Why—the shadows that drowned out the day
Are retreating! Back they flee to the womb
Of the night and eternal decay!
And what light is this from the grave where he lies?
Who comes clad in robes of eternity?
I run through the dew under morning skies—
And there is the Christ who set me free!

ENVOY

You can find him in the morning light—
You can find him in the darkest night—
He is Lord of every clime—
He is Master of all time!

Two of them went that same day to a village called Emmaus, . . . Jesus himself drew near, and went with them. But their eyes were holden that they should not know him (Luke 24:13, 15–16).

Sestina of Cleopas

Well, don't stand there—come in, come in!
We're all just brothers here that know the Lord.
You smile at that? They've told you I'm the man
Who *didn't* know the Lord himself one day?
That's right, my boy. Cleopas is my name,
And I'm the fool who muffed, O such a chance!

What a joke!—Cleopas miss a chance!
I will not boast, but I must say that in
Emmaus I've made myself, oh, quite a name,
(In business, of course). I never knew the Lord
Until two years ago, this very day.
That was the time I went to hear the man

They called Jesus. My boy, I'm not the man
For sermons, but I never missed a chance
To hear a would-be king! But on that day,
That day I heard a king—and he came in
And made himself a priest—a prophet—Lord
Of my heart—Jesus! What a name!

But there was more to him than just a name.
We couldn't tell if he was God or man.
But, in any case, I *knew* the Lord.
Sermons, miracles—I never missed a chance!
That's why it's quite a quandary I'm in—
Why I failed to know the Lord that day.

No matter that he didn't tell his name.
I'd know him in the dark! But on that day
He was a stranger. What a world we're in!
We vow our love to someone—woman or man—
But with a change of mood—a fretful chance
And we are strangers—as I was to the Lord.

Well, my boy, I've come to think the Lord
Comes often in disguise so day by day
We may be jostling God! Oh, what a chance
We take—to judge a person by his name
Or face. We're all immortal, every man!
That's the sort of world God put us in!

   ENVOY
I saw the Lord—but never knew his name.
But since that day, I look at every man.
I'll miss no other chance—when God drops in!

They [the chief priests] gave large money unto the soldiers, Saying, Say ye, His disciples came by night, and stole him away while we slept (Matt. 28:12–13).

The Bribe

How much will it cost—to keep this Jesus dead!
We have paid false witnesses to testify,
But even they could not forge a lie
Quite strong enough to drown the truth he said.

We have spent already, we chief priests,
Our honor and our sacred dignity
To stop this man, who would set all men free—
His talk of love has turned us all to beasts!

Now they say he has escaped the tomb!
But though we've paid the soldiers well to say
That his disciples stole the corpse away—
I see his shadow on the ages loom.

And all of us who murdered him are lost—
God can't be killed—even on a cross!

An Island Will Be There

I've seen the scars—like stitchings in his hands!
One glance—and there went all my plans
To get away, to leave Jerusalem.
But now he is alive!
My head's a humming hive
Of thoughts spinning wildly round my head.
Will I live a life of faith—or doubt?
Somewhere I've heard it said
A bird flies to the south;
In flocks they leave the solid land,
By faith they fly until they reach an island
That none has ever seen
Save in a heart-born dream!
Just think of that! An ounce or two of feathers
Leaving far behind its world—and trust to find a speck of green
Without a chart—without a single sign!

Is this the sort of trust
The Master asks of us?
To leave the solid guarantees of land
At his command
Believing that when our frail strength is gone
An Island will be there?
Oh, how I fear uncertainty!
And yet I think it well may be
That Christ has for his kingdom such a plan
The only man
That he could trust to use
Would be the one who'd lose
His life in a hopeless gesture!
And I—Doubting Thomas—I may now launch out
Casting aside my rags of doubt
Clad for once in faith's shining vesture!

And when he had spoken these things, while they beheld, he was taken up; and
a cloud received him out of their sight (Acts 1:9).

Cloud of Witnesses

At last—he calls! The Master calls me home!
O Gaius, his voice!—it's just the same as when
He called beside the sea: *Come, Follow me.*
And I threw down my nets and followed him.
Oh, I went splashing through the frothy sea
To him—and for three years I did not let him go.
He was my meat—my drink—I breathed his word
As prisoned slaves gulp a freshling breeze!
    And now, tonight, he calls—again:
Come, Follow me—One last time.
But—what is this? You weep, my boy?
O my son! My son! Rather leap for joy
That your old friend tonight will soar above
This Patmos, free at last from the grim cell!
This thin hand you water with your tears
Will hold tonight a nail-scarred hand,
And he I love will hold me to his breast—
As he did once before—so long ago.
That's well, my boy, you smile—
So I, before I slip away will tell
A final story—which shall it be? That one?

Well, then—

   Jesus had come back—we'd handled him
And broken bread for forty days. He'd poured
In us such love we were drunk on it.
Then, one clear day he took us to a field
Outside Jerusalem. We laughed and sang
Like children. Then he looked at us so that
We paused—and it was so still I heard a cricket
That was caught in Mary's raven hair—
He said, *Ye shall receive power.*
Be witnesses to me in all the earth.
And then—oh, my boy—he left us there!
You've watched the kestrel hawk catch a breeze,
Soar up until they vanish in the cloud?
Well, so the Master did—and what of us?
We stood there open-mouthed and vacant-headed!
That's how it was—But he had said before,
I'm coming back—Look for me each day.

   Well, then, tonight he comes for me.
All the others long ago have gone—
Only I, whom he called beloved
Has he kept in this dark place alone—
What was that? Do you not hear it, Gaius?

The air—it is alive with voices of old friends—
They call my name—that's Simon Peter there,
And Philip—there—that was Bartholomew—
And look—they are coming—all of them!
What a shining cloud of witnesses!
There is the Master—and he calls to me
In a voice that echoes through the earth:
I am come again, my faithful servant.
Come up—we are forever one!

Gilbert Morris is best known today as a novelist. His popular novels, including the American Odyssey Series, the Dani Ross Mystery Series, the House of Winslow Series, and the Appomattox Series, have sold hundreds of thousands of copies.

But Gilbert Morris is also a poet. His poetry has been published in the *Midwest Poetry Review, Texas Quarterly, Mississippi Review,* and elsewhere. While professor of English at Ouachita Baptist University, he served as president of the American Association of College Professors, as consultant for the North Central Association, and on the executive board of the National Council of Teachers of English.

He and his wife, Johnnie, reside in Bailey, Colorado, where he is writing full-time.

Illustrator Stan Myers is an award-winning artist and a member of the prestigious National Watercolor Society. His work is included in both private and corporate collections and represented by several galleries in the Midwest.